Place-Name

Chips Barber

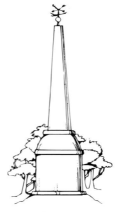

OBELISK PUBLICATIONS

ALSO BY THE AUTHOR

Around and About the Haldon Hills – Revisited • The Lost City of Exeter – Revisited
Diary of a Dartmoor Walker • Diary of a Devonshire Walker
The Great Little Dartmoor Book • The Great Little Exeter Book
The Great Little Chagford Book • The Great Little Plymouth Book
The Great Little Totnes Book • Torquay • Paignton • Brixham
Beautiful Exeter • Colourful Dartmoor • Plymouth in Colour
The South Hams in Colour • Colourful Cockington
Torbay in Colour – Torquay Paignton Brixham
Railways on and around Dartmoor • Devon's Railways of Yesteryear
Films and TV Programmes … Made in Devon
The Ghosts of Exeter • Dark and Dastardly Dartmoor • Ghastly and Ghostly Devon
Weird and Wonderful Dartmoor • Haunted Pubs in Devon
Ten Family Bike Rides in Devon
Ten Family Walks on Dartmoor • Six Short Pub Walks on Dartmoor
Ten Family Walks in East Devon • Walks on and around Woodbury Common
Topsham Past & Present • Sidmouth Past & Present • Honiton Past & Present
Along The Otter • Along The Avon • Along The Tavy
Down The Dart – Boat Trip From Totnes to Dartmouth
Sidmouth in Colour • Exmouth in Colour • Topsham in Colour
Dawlish and Dawlish Warren in Colour • Dawlish of Yesteryear
The Story of Dawlish Warren • Discovering Devon… Dawlish
From The Dart to The Start • The Story of Hallsands
Dartmouth and Kingswear • Newton Ferrers and Noss Mayo
Short Circular Walks in and around Sidmouth • Sidmouth of Yesteryear
The Dartmoor Quiz Book • Widecombe–A Visitor's Guide
Bickleigh – A Visitor's Guide • Tiverton • Plymouth Hoe • An A to Z of Devon Dialect
Around & About Salcombe • Around & About Burgh Island and Bigbury on Sea
Around & About Hope Cove and Thurlestone • Around & About Tavistock
Around & About Roborough Down • Around & About Lustleigh
Walk the East Devon Coast–Lyme Regis to Exmouth
Walk the South Devon Coast–Dawlish Warren to Dartmouth
Walk the South Hams Coast–Dartmouth to Salcombe
Walk the South Hams Coast–Salcombe to Plymouth
We have over 180 Devon titles. For full list please send SAE to
Obelisk Publications, 2 Church Hill, Pinhoe, Exeter EX4 9ER. Tel: 01392 468556.

Plate Acknowledgements
All illustrations were collected, taken or originated by Chips Barber.
Cover design by Andrea Barber.

First published in 1999
Reprinted in 2000, 2002 and 2004 by
Obelisk Publications, 2 Church Hill, Pinhoe, Exeter, Devon
Designed and Typeset by Sally Barber
Printed in Great Britain
by Avocet Press, Cullompton, Devon

Place-Names in Devon

Place-names and their meanings, if they have any, are a constant source of enjoyment (or frustration) and a knowledge of them can be educational, particularly when there is a 'story' behind them. People are often curious or amused by how a place – be it pub, hill, headland, wood, farm, hamlet, village, town or city – derived its name. This book is more of a fun book than a comprehensive gazetteer, because interpreting place-names is an inexact science. Indeed it's important to stress that many names, if not the majority, are open to debate, and this book should not be taken as 'gospel'. The roots of many place-names were planted long ago and their precise origins have been largely obscured by the mists of time. Many names originate from the founder of the original settlement, which would have been a 'farm', but not in the visual sense as we know them today. These personal names, so common in place-names, are obscure and, of course, there are few records to show exactly what they were. It is only those with a knowledge of ancient languages and etymology who can even begin to make plausible guesses as to what they might

have been all those centuries ago. Those who wish for a more disciplined, academic approach should consult full, detailed texts like *The Place-Names of Devon* by J. E. B. Gover, A. Mawer, and F. M. Stenton, which was published by the Cambridge University Press in 1931. It was a most useful source of information when compiling this book. It is found in some reference libraries, is in two volumes and is a comprehensive guide dealing with the names of thousands of farms and hamlets. Occasional copies which turn up in specialist second-hand bookshops command very high prices.

Being given the briefest, possibly even the loosest suggestion as to what many names might mean may perhaps lead you to do further, more detailed research on specific place-names which may interest you. After all, 'What's in a name?' I didn't start life with the name 'Chips', and you might think I was a carpenter, or I spent a lot of time in casinos – or perhaps I ate too many French fries? Names are not always obvious.

Size of settlement is not important; some of the tiniest places have longer explanations than many of the bigger ones! Unless you have an encyclopaedic knowledge of Devon, one of the largest

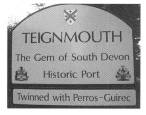

counties in England, you may not have heard of many of these places. On occasions I have tried to give a brief mention of the whereabouts of some of the smaller, lesser-known ones. I appreciate that people in the south of the county may well be familiar with their own 'patch' but that 'in the wilds' of Mid or North Devon they may be 'lost'. And the same applies for those who have the good fortune to live in those wilds, for you may never have ventured down into some of the creeks and valleys of the warmer and more sheltered southern parts of the county. I hope the book reasonably covers all of Devon as far as the distribution of place-names is concerned. I apologise if I have left out or ignored the ones which you want to know. This then, is just a selection of the many thousands of names found in Devon. Some names have been recorded without definition because they are just so lovely or quaint.

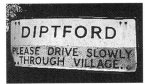

The illustrations for this book are really as much for design as for their artistic or academic value, as they are intended to break up the pages of type. Having photographed many village and town name signs,I notice that there is a growing tendency to add more and more information, such as twin towns (and some places have several!) or the nature of the town: 'Regency resort' 'Stannary town' and so on. It's all just part of the name game and a mild example of marketing! Some of these signs, which cost a lot of money to make and install, could not be photographed because they were covered in layers of grime and dirt. Diptford, in the Avon valley, had one which was bent and buckled. Not surprisingly in a county with many churches, and where there once were as many monasteries as today there are holiday camps, we start and end with religious settlements …

ABBOT'S BICKINGTON, a tiny place, with a miniature church, in north-west Devon, was part of the original endowment of the nearby Hartland Abbey.

ABBOTSHAM, near Bideford, also has a definitely ecclesiastical feel to its name and rightly so, because it was developed out of the tenth century endowment of Tavistock Abbey.

ABBOTSKERSWELL (sometimes written Abbot's Kerswell) is yet another place with religious overtones in its name. Land in this area was held by the Abbot of Horton (once in Dorset, now in Somerset) in 1086. The 'Kerswell' part of the name, so common in this part of the county, refers to the bountiful springs of fresh water found there, essential for any settlement to thrive. Thus the interpretation seems to be 'the spring on the Abbot's land where cress grows'.

ALFARDISWORTHY rarely gets a mention in any book, and the majority of people in South Devon have never heard of this small place in the northern part of the county which, like many others, probably derives its name from its founder, in this case 'Alfheard'.

ALLER BROOK is a tributary of the Teign, joining it below the Newton Abbot by-pass flyover, and means 'alder', a tree which thrives in damp conditions.

ALPHINGTON, part of Exeter, was 'the farm of Alpha' but is now a suburb. This 'village' takes its name from the Alphin Brook, one that flooded the nether regions of the city on numerous occasions before being canalised or placed in a deep, wide concrete trough, in its lower reaches.

ALVERDISCOTT, in North Devon, pronounced Alscott, was the settlement of Aelfweard.

ANSTEY is a common name in Devon, which is not surprising in so hilly a county as this means 'path up a hill'. Examples include Anstey's Barrow (East Anstey), Anstey's Gate (West Anstey) and Anstey's Cove (Torquay). However, an alternative meaning for the latter is 'narrow cove'. It is certainly not wide and has proved to be a suitable spot for smuggling even in recent times!

APPLEDORE may well originally have been called 'Tawmutha', the place at the mouth of the River Taw. Certainly had it done so it would have followed the pattern of many Devonshire ports at mouths of rivers, as will be obvious if this book is read thoroughly! The Old English word for apple is 'apuldor' and so this is possibly 'the place by the apple-tree'.

ASH is common in Devon and many farms, hamlets, villages and towns have used the association with this type of tree. Apart from at least six settlements simply called 'Ash', there are also five Ashridges. Listed below are just a handful of those prefixed with 'Ash'.

ASHBURN is the name of a short river, also known as the Yeo, which rises on Eastern Dartmoor and flows steeply down to join the Dart at Buckfastleigh. As in Scotland, a 'burn' in Devon is a stream. It is 'the stream where the ash-tree flourishes'.

ASHBURTON, on the banks of the Ashburn, is an ancient stannary town which derives its name from the river. Variations in this settlement's spelling, throughout the years, include Essebretona at Domesday followed by Aschperton, Ashperton and Assheburton.

ASHBURY, near Okehampton, is 'the fort by the ash tree'.

ASHCOMBE, on the edge of Haldon, near Dawlish, is 'the valley of ash trees'.

ASHFORD, near the Taw estuary, is 'the crossing place in the ash wood'.

ASHPRINGTON, near Totnes, was Asprinton in 1086 and is probably 'the farm of Aesheorht'.

ASHREIGNEY is a hilltop village, between Dartmoor and Exmoor. It is believed that 'locals' called it Rings Ash whilst the gentry preferred to call it Ashreigney. There is reputed to be a stone in the parish which is marked 'Ashreney also Ringsash'. Its name is from an Old English word which means 'ash tree'. The family of 'Regny' was first here in 1219 and 'Rings' is believed to be a corruption of their name.

ATHERINGTON, in North Devon, was probably 'Eadhere's farm'.

ATMOSPHERIC RAILWAY is the name of a pub at Starcross on the Exe Estuary. Its name refers to a system of railway engine propulsion that Brunel used from Exeter southwards along the estuary and round the coast of this part of South Devon. It involved the building of 'pumping houses' every three miles. One of the few to survive is nearby. The system, which was problematic, was dropped in favour of a more conventional form of locomotion.

AUSEWELL ROCKS, which may mean 'aspen spring', are in private woodlands above the Dart near Ashburton. In 1606 the name given for this location was Apswell Rock.

AVETON GIFFORD, in the heart of the South Hams, is pronounced, by some, as Awton Jifford (it was Awton Gifford in 1546!) although this often causes heated arguments as there are various ways of saying the place-name. It means 'the farm by the Avon'. The first part of the name is obviously a corruption of Avon, whilst the second element is derived from the family who owned vast tracts of land here long ago.

AVON is a common Celtic name for a river in England for the good reason that it means 'river'. Several other counties have a River Avon. A popular variation of the name of this particular Avon is Aune, and along this lovely river's banks are many places like Aunemouth.

AVONWICK, near South Brent, was named 'Newhouse' until about 1870.

AXE means 'water', as in Axmouth and Axminster in East Devon.

AXMINSTER is famous for its carpets. The Axe is the river and the 'minster', an important church, was founded soon after the year 705, when the see or diocese of Sherborne was created to bring Devon in line with episcopal organisation. The large parish church of St Mary and St John the Evangelist is still the most obvious landmark in this small East Devon town.

AWLISCOMBE, near Honiton, is in the valley of the River Wolf. It has been suggested that the Wolf was once called the Awl but there is no proof of this. Others believe that the first part of the name means 'forked', relating to two streams which, if you look at a detailed map, do fork here. The heart of the village sits above their confluence.

AYLESBEARE, in East Devon, probably comes from 'Aegel's wood' and it was from here that the famous Tommy Cooper got his first magic set, a gift from an aunt.

BABBACOMBE takes its name from its probable founder, 'Babba'. 'Combe' means 'valley'. The original settlement was close to sea level, where Babbacombe Quay is located.

BALL on Dartmoor appears in many names and refers to rounded hills. Examples include Hemerdon Ball, Cuckoo Ball and Corringdon Ball, near South Brent.

BAMPTON, north of Tiverton, stands on the River Batherm. It is just possible that it means something like 'farm of the dwellers by the pool'.

BANK, preceded by the word 'The', is a pub in Plymouth located behind the Theatre Royal and beside 'Derry's Clock', named after William Derry, former Mayor of Plymouth. The Bank was once a real bank and still possesses the architectural appearance of one. This small picture shows both the clock and Lloyds Bank as it looked in 1934, before the Plymouth blitz destroyed the buildings on the left side of the scene.

BARBICAN occurs a few times in Devon: in a flight of steps against Exeter's Roman wall; it gives its name to one of the older parts of Plymouth; and is also found in Barnstaple. It means 'a fortified place', usually an outer defence work.

BARNSTAPLE, alias 'Barum', 'the capital of North Devon', grew at the meeting point of the important Taw and the smaller Yeo because the Taw was fordable. Its name probably means 'Bearda's staple or post'. It is possible that these 'bearded posts' enabled vessels to navigate the tidal River Taw. Barnstaple is one of the most misspelt names in Devon, when the antepenultimate letter becomes a 'b' rather than a 'p'!

BARTON crops up, if you'll excuse the pun, several times in Devon. It was often the place where a farmer stored his barley or one which served all the small farms of a district.

BEACONS were set up on the highest hills and used in times of emergency to warn of invasion. A network existed, so that the entire country could be alerted in a short time. However, one set off by mistake could have caused panic for several days. Many high points are called Beacon Hill and the name has been adopted for many house and farm names.

BEAFORD is near Great Torrington, by gad. Unlikely as it may sound, it is possibly the place where the blood-sucking 'gad-fly' annoyed cattle near a ford.

BEAWORTHY, in mid-Devon, is possibly from 'Beaga's farm', an Anglo-Saxon worthy.

BECKA or BECKY is found in Becka Brook and also in Becka or Becky Falls. It derives from the northern word 'beck', meaning 'a little stream with a rocky bottom'.

BEER is an attractive East Devon fishing village that boasts my favourite place-name but, alas, it has little to do with the drink! It, like other Beers, Beares and Beres, is of a woody disposition, although today you would never think so. The Beer Brook, now flowing beside the main street, would have tumbled seawards through a wooded valley at one time.

BEESANDS, a delightful fishing village near Start Point, was 'Base Sande' in 1514.

BELSTONE is a beautiful village of quaint granite cottages on the northern edge of Dartmoor. It is possibly named after a logan-stone, a rock precariously balanced that could rock or 'log' when pressure was applied to certain points. This one was said to 'roll like a ship in a gale'. However, it rocked too far and the fallen rocks were broken up by quarrymen and removed, so it's said. *The Belstone Fox* (1973) is not related to this village.

BERE FERRERS (see also Ferrers) is a small settlement close to the point where the River Tavy flows into the 'mighty Tamar'. Its name possibly derives from 'birland' meaning a spit or point which, if you look at a map to show its location, is appropriate. Some translations make it 'the fortified freehold of the Ferrers family'. In the past it was commonly called 'Beertown'.

BERRYNARBOR is a lovely, award-winning village near Ilfracombe. In the fourteenth century two wealthy families in this district, the Berrys and the Nerberts, were linked by marriage. The settlement became Berry Nerbert but corrupted to Berry Narbor in the seventeenth century.

BERRY POMEROY, near Totnes, is a small village, about a half-mile from the castle of the same name. This is, quite possibly, the most haunted ruin in the kingdom! Berry, like bury, burgh, and burh, indicates the presence of a fort or stronghold of some kind. In this instance it was the one belonging to the Pomeroys, who owned the area from the thirteenth century (and their ghosts are still with us!). The wedding scene at the end of the 1990s film version of *Sense and Sensibility* was filmed at the church in the village.

BICKINGTON, near Ashburton, means either 'Beocca's farm' or 'the town on the brook', this being the River Lemon which, lower down its valley, 'squeezes' through Newton Abbot.

BICKINGTON, in North Devon, was possibly 'the farm where the bees nest'.

BICKLEIGH is also found twice in Devon, once near Plymouth and again about four miles to the south of Tiverton in the Exe valley. One interpretation is 'Bicca's clearing' but some sources suggest that the Exe valley Bickleigh means 'a place of cows'.

BICTON, in East Devon, is possibly 'Bica's farm' or 'Beocca's farm'.

BIDEFORD is a Saxon settlement deriving from 'Byda's ford', after a man, no doubt, of ancient lineage who possibly found a way of crossing the tidal river waters of the Torridge without drowning himself or his compatriots. Charles Kingsley, who wrote parts of his famous *Westward Ho!* when staying at a hotel in this port, described it as 'the little white town', which seems fitting even today with so many whitewashed buildings adorning the steep hillsides.

BIGBURY and **BIGBURY-ON-SEA** are separate places, the former a mile inland, the latter a modern resort opposite Burgh Island, at the mouth of the Avon. Bigbury means 'Bicca's fort'.

BISHOP BLAIZE is the name of a pub close to Exeter Quay. He was the patron saint of the wool trade and all the 'court' names nearby are also to commemorate Exeter's once important woollen trade. These include Dyers Court, Carders Court, Fullers Court, Shearman Court, Serge Court and Teazle Court. Would I try to pull the wool over your eyes?

BISHOP'S NYMPTON, in North Devon, was an estate held by the Bishop of Exeter in 1086.

BISHOP'S TAWTON, it is believed, was where the 'Bishop of Devon' once had his 'HQ', before it moved to Crediton and thence to Exeter. The land was held by the Bishop of Exeter in 1086. The Tawton refers to 'the stockaded farm by the river Taw', a river which runs close by.

BISHOPSTEIGNTON belonged to the bishops of Exeter, from 1086, and here you will find the ruins, on a farm, of one of their former palaces.

BLACK precedes a lot of names on Dartmoor and often refers to the presence of peat, which covers many square miles of moorland. Examples include the romantic-sounding (!) Black Dunghill, Black Lane, Black Hole and so on.

BLACK DOG, a hamlet 'in the middle of nowhere', is most unusual in that it is named after its local, the Black Dog pub. The spectre of a ghostly black dog is a common sight in this part of Devon. You will not be regarded as 'barking mad' if you see it!

BLACK TORRINGTON is near Hatherleigh. The first part is believed to be a description of the River Torridge, which is supposed to show a hint or tint of black here.

BLACKAWTON was one of the evacuated villages of the South Hams where the Americans 'rehearsed' for D-day. The 'black' part of the name may refer to the slates found locally, which are black, and blacker still when wet, after rain. 'Awton' probably means 'Afa's farm'.

BLACKBOROUGH, which probably means 'dark hill', is high on the edge of the Blackdown Hills which straddle the Devon/Somerset border. They, perversely, are sometimes referred to as the Whitestone Hills. 'Whet stone' was quarried at Blackborough until 1932.

BLACKBURY CASTLE, in East Devon, meaning 'black earth-work', is an ancient hill fort.

BONDLEIGH, in mid-Devon, is possibly derived from 'Bola's clearing'.

BORINGDON, at Plympton, may well mean 'fortified hill'.

BOVEY TRACEY is pronounced 'Buvvy'. It has been mooted that 'Bovey' comes from a Saxon theign called Boui or Bofa. Henry de Tracey formed a borough here in the thirteenth century.

BOW is between Crediton and Okehampton and possibly its name relates to the shape of an arched bridge over the Yeo. I always chuckle when driving through it because, according to the village sign it tells us that 'Bow', one of the shortest place-names in the county, is twinned with St Martin de Bienfaite La Cressoniere! That's the long and short of it, or vice-versa. Bow replaced 'Nymet Tracey', 'a decayed town'. The latter had a market granted to Henry de Tracey in 1258, so he was obviously a man of great substance.

BOWD is a hamlet, with a pub of the same name, on the outskirts of Sidmouth. This name possibly means 'beneath or under the hill' and that's precisely where it is located, because rising sharply above it are Beacon Hill, Core Hill, and Bulverton Hill. Another suggested meaning is 'curved wood', and nearby is Harpford Wood, which may be the one in question.

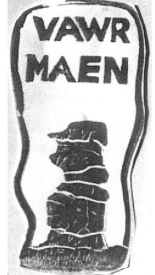

BOWERMAN'S NOSE is a queer rock idol on Dartmoor, on the side of Hayne Down, not far from Hound Tor. It is a rock with a legend that says that this is a giant who was turned to stone, after being ambushed, by three witches whom he had upset. The ancient name for this rock is Vawr Maen meaning 'great stone' or 'giant rock'. The illustration shows part of the original 'letter-box' stamp.

BOYTON, in the Tamar valley, means 'homestead or farm in the wood'.

BRADDON occurs in many hill names and probably means 'broad hill'.

BRADFORD is a small village in North Devon and not the great Yorkshire town of the same name. Its name derives from its location at a crossing-place over the Torridge, a useful 'broad ford'.

BRADNINCH, the Duchy 'town' of East Devon, is believed to mean a 'broad ash tree'.

BRADSTONE means 'at the broad stone', possibly from one near the church!

BRADWORTHY, in north-west Devon, roughly means 'broad space' or 'broad estate', which is appropriate as the village square is one of record dimensions.

BRAMPFORD SPEKE, 'the ford by the brambles', is on a bluff above the River Exe, a few miles outside Exeter. The second part relates to the Speke family; Captain Speke was in the expedition which discovered the source of the Nile. According to Worth's *History of Devonshire* (1886) *'There is a tradition that certain paths in Devon were appropriated for the sole use of the Spekes, and hence called Speke-paths'.*

BRANDIS CORNER is just to the north of Whiddon Down. The dialect phrase 'brandis-wise' means 'in the shape of a triangle' and the OS map shows an obvious triangle of roads here.

BRANSCOMBE, a sprawling East Devon village in a deep combe or valley, made up of many small clusters of buildings, takes its name from a Celt called Brannoc.

BRATTON CLOVELLY lies just to the north of Dartmoor. Bratton possibly means 'a strip of uncultivated land'. The second part of its name is derived from the Claville family.

BRAUNTON in a breezy part of North Devon has evolved from a word meaning 'the farm in the broom', this being of the woody variety and nothing to do with sweeping implements! However another translation was offered in Worth's *History of Devonshire* (1886) *'Braunton, presumably derived from Brannock's "tun", Brannock being the patron saint; and the legend of ... the church (is) that he was directed to build it where he next saw a sow and her litter, in witness whereof sow and farrows are to be seen duly carven on a boss'.*

BRENTOR is a very steep hill and that's precisely what it means as well! There are many steep hills in the country with a similar name, the other most obvious example in this region being Brent Knoll, a similarly distinct hill rising above the M5 and the flat levels of the Somerset countryside.

BRIDESTOWE has nothing to with brides! 'Stow' means 'holy place' and in this case it was the shrine of St Brigid or 'Bride', to whom the church in this moorland-edge village is dedicated. As most good Irishmen will tell you she was a famous saint who lived from about 450 to 525. She is depicted in a window as an old lady carrying lilies.

BRIDFORD is possibly 'ford of the young birds' or probably 'bride's ford'.

BRIDGERULE, in west Devon, takes its name from 'the bridge of Ruald'.

BRIM BROOK, found on Dartmoor and elsewhere, means 'bramble brook'.

BRIMLEY, meaning 'a clearing in the broom', is now a part of Bovey Tracey.

BRIMPTS is the 'bramble-grown hill' and rises above Dartmeet on Dartmoor. Today it is inhabited by pixies but is largely covered in trees, Brimpts Plantation!

BRIXHAM is a famous fishing port which takes its name from a Celt called Brioc who built his

homestead here long ago. In a 1960s feature film, *The System,* which starred the late Oliver Reed, several scenes were filmed in the port, which became 'Wroxham' for the Big Screen. In Higher Brixham you will find 'Paddiwack Cottage' in Knick Knack Lane. Give the dog a bone!

BRIXTON, near Plymouth, like Brixham, probably stems from Brioc.

BROADCLYST is located in a broad part of the Clyst valley but the river, here, is narrow!

BROADHEMBURY, one of Devon's prettiest villages, is near the famous hill fort of Hembury. It means 'high place' but this village lies at the base of the hills.

BROADWOOD KELLY, near Hatherleigh, was the 'wide wood' held by William de Kelly in 1242.

BROADWOODWIDGER, which stands above the valley of the River Wolf overlooking Dartmoor, is 'the broad wood', once of the Wyger family, who were there in 1273.

BRUSHFORD, in mid-Devon, can be translated as 'bridge ford'.

BUCKFASTLEIGH is a wonderfully spelt place name for it uses exactly half the alphabet without repeating a letter! The first part of the name alludes to the deer which once roamed here, and the rest tells us that it was in a forest clearing where they took shelter or simply gathered. There are no 'Bambis' in Buckfastleigh now!

In Buckfastleigh you will find 'Elliott Plain'. This is not a flat thoroughfare but a place-name which is derived from an author whose pen-name this was. Born locally, his real name was Walter Holdsworth (1881–1946) and his books were set in this area. He often built his stories around local tales, one of them being a variation on the Widecombe Fair saga.

BUCKLAND, in general terms, is usually land held by a charter from the King. By the nature of this it was recorded in a book, so it's 'Book-land'!

BUCKLAND BREWER, in North Devon, is a corruption of Briwerre, who was the Lord of the Manor in the first years of the thirteenth century.

BUCKLAND-IN-THE-MOOR, another village of picture-postcard cottages, is distinguished from other Bucklands by its location on or in-the-moor. This village is famous for two unusual inscriptions. High on the hill above is Buckland Beacon, a tremendous vantage point. Mr Whitley, Lord of the Manor in 1928, singled out two rocks which he felt resembled the two tablets God gave to Moses and had Arthur Clement carve the Ten Commandments on them. This was done to celebrate the defeat in Parliament, in 1928, of a proposed revised edition of the prayer book. On the clock-face of the church in the village, instead of numerals 1 to 12 we find the words 'My Dear Mother' spelt out, a further example of Whitley devotion.

BUCKLAND MONACHORUM features in some rhyming doggerel: "If you want to stagger 'em say Monaggorum, but if you want decorum say Monochorum". It means 'of the monks', and the nearby Buckland Abbey, founded in 1278, former home of Sir Francis Drake, was an important monastery until the Dissolution. Now it is a National Trust property.

BUCKLAND TOUT SAINTS, near Kingsbridge, is a quiet, off-the-beaten-track place. Tout Saints is not, as I thought, 'All Saints', but a corruption of the name of a thirteenth century family who were the Lords of the Manor. Their name was de Tuz Seinz!

BUDLEIGH SALTERTON, the retirement capital of East Devon, sometimes referred to by locals, only jokingly, as 'God's Waiting Room', is a long name. It is believed that 'locals' simply say 'Salterton' as 'Budleigh' refers to East Budleigh, a mile or two inland. The latter part of the name relates to the former salt-pans in the nearby Otter estuary.

BULKWORTHY, in the upper Torridge valley, was possibly 'Bulca's farm'.

BULL HILL is a big sand bank in the Exe Estuary. It is so named because it is in the shape of a bull, as is seen on detailed maps today or from an aeroplane when the tide is out.

BURGH ISLAND is wonderful! It sits at the mouth of the Avon and was known as 'la Burgh' in the fifteenth century.

BURLESCOMBE, near the Somerset border, could mean 'Burgweald's valley'.

BURRINGTON, 'in the wilds of North Devon', and birthplace of my accountant, may mean 'peasant's farm'. How inappropriate!

BUTTERLEIGH, 'utterly' in the hills between Silverton and Tiverton, is where Salman Rushdie wrote one of his books. It means 'a clearing with rich pasture land'.

BUTTS PARK is a name commonly found in Devon. The village green at Widecombe is just one example. The 'Butt' refers to a target at which arrows were fired. In 1466, during the reign of Edward II, it was decreed that ' ... every Englishman should have a bow of his own height of yew, ash, wych, hazel, or amburn: and that butts should be made in every township, which the inhabitants were to shoot at every feast-day under penalty of a ha'penny ...'.

CADBURY is a small village and hill fort on the side of the Exe Valley and its name has nothing to do with chocolate! It is probably 'Cada's camp'.

CADELEIGH, the next parish to Cadbury, is derived from the same 'Cada'.

CADMUS ROCKS are located near Salcombe and at the mouth of the Kingsbridge Estuary. In June 1869 HMS *Cadmus*, whilst en route between Portsmouth and Devonport, went aground here in dense fog but was later refloated and taken away for repairs. Locals then endowed the previously unnamed rocks with the ship's name.

CADOVER BRIDGE, on south-western Dartmoor, spans the River Plym at a beauty spot. Some claim that the moorland part of the Plym was called the Cad, so Cadover Bridge begins to make sense! However, it is believed that it is from 'coed weorthig', 'the farm-place in the wood'.

CAREY, a tributary of the Tamar, probably means 'friendly, pleasant stream'.

CASTLE usually conjures up an image of drawbridges, portcullises, towers, ramparts and so on but in Devon, more often than not, many of the 'castles' named on maps are simply Iron Age 'hill forts'. Examples include Cranbrook, Prestonbury, Woolston, in the Teign Valley and Woodbury and Sidbury in East Devon. However, there are some grander, later edifices that reflect the true spirit of castles and these include Totnes and Okehampton.

CATTEDOWN and also Cattewater are problematic Plymouth place-names and even disciplined historians have struggled to explain them. It's possible that the origins of these names hark back to the times of one of the Danish invasions. It is possible that 'Catte' has a similar root to the Kattegat (verbal partner of Skaggerak), a channel between Denmark and Sweden.

CALVERLEIGH is 'the clearing in the bare wood'.

CHADDLEWOOD, now part of Plympton, may mean 'the cold spring in the wood'.

CHAGFORD, dwarfed by the gigantic Meldon Hill, and one of the best places in Devon, means 'gorse ford'. This ancient stannary town, in the north-eastern quadrant of Dartmoor, is on rising ground above a fording place on the River Teign.

CHALLABOROUGH is a small seaside resort, mainly of caravans now, close to Bigbury-on-Sea. It means 'the peasants' fortified hill'.

CHALLACOMBE is quite common in Devon and means 'cold valley'.

CHARDSTOCK is possibly 'the stock farm belonging to Chard', a person.

CHAWLEIGH, a small place near Chulmleigh, means 'calves' clearing'.

CHERITON BISHOP lies close to the A30 Exeter to Okehampton road but is by-passed these days. The first part of the name means either 'farm by the church' or 'church town', and the 'Bishop' part establishes an episcopal connection.

CHERITON FITZPAINE has the same root but is qualified by the addition of Fitzpaine, after the family who held the manor in the thirteenth century.

CHERRYBROOK is a lovely tributary of the Dart. Its waters once powered the waterwheels at the Powder Mills, a nineteenth century gunpowder factory near Postbridge on Dartmoor. Its name possibly means 'winding or twisting river'.

CHIPSHOP is a mining hamlet between the Tamar and Tavistock. 'Chips' were tokens issued by mining companies to supplement miners' wages. They could only be spent in the 'Chipshop'.

CHITTLEHAMHOLT, in North Devon, was a hamlet of Chittlehampton and was probably evolved out of a forest clearing, or 'holt' as it was termed in this instance.

CHITTLEHAMPTON, in North Devon, probably means 'the dwellers' farm in the hollow'.

CHIVELSTONE, on the opposite side of the estuary to Salcombe, is probably 'Ceofel's farm'.

CHOLAKE, a small Dartmoor stream, probably means 'cold brook'.

CHOLWICH TOWN, near Cornwood, means 'coldest farm'.

CHRISTOW, on a hill above the Teign valley, is 'a place dedicated to Christ'.

CHUDLEIGH, also on a hill above the Teign valley, but a few miles further south was, originally, 'Chud's settlement' and developed in a clearing of a wood. 'Chudleys' are semi-sweet yeast buns which sometimes have been used instead of more traditional scones in cream teas.

CHULMLEIGH, where the first 'l' remains silent, possibly means 'Ceolmund's clearing'.

CHURCHSTOW was once a possession of the earlier and original Buckfast Abbey. Like Christow, Instow and Morwenstow, it is a religious name; its church is the dominant landmark. This small village, high above the Avon valley, was once a more important place than it is today.

CHURSTON FERRERS, near Brixham, is 'the church farm'. Hugo de Fereris held the land in 1303.

CLANNABOROUGH, near Copplestone in Mid-Devon, and also found as a place-name near Throwleigh on Dartmoor, supposedly means 'cloven hill'.

CLAWTON is 'the farm by the River Claw', a tributary of the River Tamar. Its name may refer to a tongue of land in the shape of a claw.

CLAYHANGER is, most probably, 'a wood on a steep-sided hill of clay'.

CLAYHIDON, in East Devon, may mean 'hay hill' or 'clay hill'.

CLEARBROOK, a hamlet near Yelverton, on the side of Roborough Down, is where you will find a 'clear brook', which flows into the River Meavy.

CLEAVE means a steep-sided valley, of which there are many in Devon. Examples on Dartmoor are Belstone, Lustleigh and Tavy cleaves.

CLOVELLY, one of the biggest tourist attractions in the county, may derive from the Latin 'Clausa Vallis' meaning 'the closed glen', or it may come from the Saxon language and mean 'cliff place' or 'ravine'.

CLYST is a small river in East Devon, a tributary of the River Exe, which gives its name to a number of settlements, mostly small, along its course. These include several which are distinguished by adding the name of the church dedication, examples being Clyst St Mary, Clyst St George and Clyst St Lawrence. Clyst William is where the river rises. Clyst Hydon was a manor which was owned by Ricardus de Hidune in 1242. Clyst Honiton is beside the main Exeter to Honiton road, and there is much debate as to whether it's more correct to call it Honiton Clyst. However, all maps bear the former name. One 'Clyst' which did not survive as a parish was 'Clyst Fomison' which is now part of Sowton parish. 'Clyst' means 'clear stream' which, if you say it quickly enough, sounds like this name. In its lower reaches it is prone to flooding. At such times it is  anything but clear, with much red earth sediment in it making it very brown. It is one of a few rivers in the county to have had levees built along it long ago. Whenever the origin of Devonshire place-names is discussed, this is the one name that is always put forward for interpretation and one of the easiest and most straightforward to explain.

COCKINGTON is yet another 'picture postcard village' of thatched cottages and gift shops. The first part of its name means 'red', and if you see the colour of ploughed fields in the vicinity you will appreciate the place-name's aptness. It's 'a farm on red earth'.

COFFINSWELL, near Newton Abbot, has nothing to do with funerals! Hugo de Coffin held the manor in 1285 and, no doubt, there is a spring there.

COFTON, near Starcross, means 'red farm' owing to the soil colour.

COLATON RALEIGH had the second part of its name, after the famous local family, added to help differentiate it from Colyton farther east, also in East Devon. It derives from 'Cola's farm', a large farm. Wimundus de Ralegh held the manor in 1242.

COLDRIDGE is, as its name suggests, situated on a 'cold ridge'.

COLEBROOKE, or Colebrook, near Crediton, is possibly the 'cool brook' but there aren't any warm ones in Devon! Another interpretation is 'Cola's Brook' so is this the secret ingredient of a world-famous drink? I think not!

COLUMBJOHN is a hamlet in the lower Culm valley on the edge of the NT property of Killerton. Its name probably means something like 'the manor of John by the river Culm'.

COLYFORD, in East Devon, means 'the crossing place over the River Coly'. Coly = narrow.

COLYTON is the 'farm by the river Coly', another East Devon river prone to flooding.

COMBE means a 'valley' and in a hilly county like Devon there are many in the landscape. Villages that have developed in them often have the word 'combe' somewhere in the name. Examples include Widecombe, Combe Martin, Ilfracombe, Branscombe and so on. Combe or Coombe, as a name in itself, usually for farms, appears more than 80 times on Devonshire maps.

COMBE MARTIN, a small but extremely long seaside resort in North Devon, is also in a valley. 'Martin' was added when the land was passed over to Martyn de Tours. It is interesting to note that the river which runs down this valley is called the Umber because this substance was extracted from it. Silver mines, now derelict, are found on the hillside.

COMBEINTEIGNHEAD is located in the valley of a small stream which issues into the Teign estuary between Newton Abbot and Shaldon. It means 'in the valley of the Ten Hides'.

COMBPYNE, in an East Devon valley, was, in the thirteenth century, owned by the de Pyn family. Sir Thomas de Pyn was the patron of the local church in 1278.

COMMON NAMES in Devon are numerous. Many relate to places which derive their names from their situation. In a list of farms, hamlets, and villages of the county many appear with amazing frequency. So we find Ash 19 times, Beara 16, Beer or Beera 16, Berry 14, Birch 14, Borough 9, Bowden 19, Brimley 7, Brook 12, Buckland 6, Burrow 13, Combe or Coombe 81, Croft 7, Eastacott 10, Ford or Forda 56, Heathfield 12, Hele 18, Holcombe 6, Hole 30, Holland 5, Holwell 12, Honeywell 5, Horridge 6, Kerswell 6, Knap or Knapp 8, Knowle 22, Lake 19, Langdon 8, Langford 8, Langley 5, Lee 12, Leigh 16, Ley 12, Little Silver 8, Luscombe 5, Marsh 11, Merrifield 7, Middlecott 9, Milltown 5, Moortown 8, Narracott 10, Nethercott 12, Netherton 8, Newland or Newlands 9, Northcott 6, Northdown 6, North Wood or Northwood 9, Norton 6, Orchard 6, Pit or Pitt 22, Pool or Poole 14, Ranscombe 5, Ridge 7, Rowden 9, Rull 7, Shilston or Shilstone 8, Shortacombe 5, Shute 6, Slade 18, Smallacombe 5, Southcott 12, Southdown 7, South Wood or Southwood 9, Staddon 6, Stone 21, Stowford 12, Thorn or Thorne 22, Torr 8, Town 7, Upcott 37, Upton 8, Venn 30, Waterhouse 6, Way or Waye 12, Waytown 6, Week or Weeke 23, Well 15, Westcott or Westacott 26, Weston 7, Whiddon 7, Whitely or Whitly 6, Whitestone 5, Winscott 5, Wood 17, Woodhouse 12, Woodland or Woodlands 12, Woodtown 5, Wotton 5, Yard or Yarde 11, Yelland 6, Yeo 20, and Zeal 5 times. No wonder post often goes astray in Devon!

COPPA DOLLA, 'the pollarded alder', is the name of a pub and a farm at Broadhempston.

COPPICETOWN, near Roborough Down, means 'Copper's town'.

COPPLESTONE, on the Crediton to Barnstaple road, takes its name from a ten feet high, tenth century boundary stone where three parishes, Crediton, Down St Mary and Colebrook, are joined. The charter of 974 refers to the 'copelan stan', which may well mean 'the chief stone'.

CORBYN'S HEAD is a much-eroded sandstone promontory at the southern end of Torre Abbey Sands in Torquay. It's name is believed to mean 'the crooked headland' although some suggest 'carved headland' and even 'cut nose of land', whatever that means!

CORNWOOD, on the edge of south-western Dartmoor, means 'crane wood'.

CORYTON is probably 'the farm by the Cory'.

COUNTISBURY, rising steeply from Lynmouth, means 'fort on the hill or headland'.

COUNTESS WEAR is now a suburb of Exeter. Its name is derived from a powerful lady, Isabella de Fortibus, Countess of Devon, who blocked the Exe here with a weir, in 1286, thereby effectively stopping ships from travelling up river to Exeter Quay. The Courtenays (Earls of Devon) owned the port of Topsham and benefited from the landing dues there. Goods had then to be carried to Exeter by packhorse teams along 'Topsham Road'. Although the weir was removed in the time of Henry VIII the river had silted up, so the first Exeter Canal was constructed to sidestep the former obstruction. (See also **RING-IN-THE-MIRE.**)

CRANMERE POOL is the subject of one of my books. It is nothing more than an empty hollow with a letterbox, the most famous on Dartmoor, sited on its edge. Since 1854, this empty 'mountain tarn', in the heart of a wilderness, high on the Northern Moors, has been a place of pilgrimage for thousands of walkers. Even 'Tarka the Otter' (and author Henry Williamson) has visited 'the pool'. However, it's another creature, the crane, which gives its name to the pool. But why not read the book?

CRAZYWELL POOL, again on Dartmoor but high on the side of one of the valleys feeding Burrator Lake, is an old mine working filled with water and is haunted. (See *Dark & Dastardly Dartmoor.*) Its name has evolved through a number of earlier versions which include Classenwell and Classiewell. The 'well' is obvious but the first part remains another mystery of the moor.

CREACOMBE, one of the remotest parishes in North Devon, means 'crow valley'.

CREDITON, an ancient and famous town, is 'the farm by the River Creedy.'

CREEDY, which gives its name to Crediton, is believed to mean 'winding' or 'twisting'.

CROWNHILL, in Plymouth, dates back to about 1880. There has been a suggestion that this 'new name' was adopted when the area developed. The original name was 'Knackersknowle'!

CRUWYS MORCHARD was the seat of the Cruwys family from the twelfth century. Cruwys derives from an old word meaning 'cross'. Morchard means 'the great wood'.

CULLOMPTON means 'farm on the River Culm'.

CULM may mean that it's another twisting or 'knotted river'.

CULMSTOCK is possibly 'the stock farm on the River Culm'.

DADDYHOLE PLAIN at Torquay may derive from the old Devonshire word for the Devil, i.e. 'Daddy'. Thus this is the 'Demon's Cave', situated below the flat-topped cliff.

DALWOOD is 'the wood in the valley'.

DAMAREL appears in many place-names, particularly in the Plymouth area. It often indicates a link with the D'Albemarle family.

DARTINGTON is 'a farm by the Dart' and is now principally a seat of learning.

DARTMEET is a well-known beauty spot where the rivers East and West Dart meet.

DARTMOOR takes its name from 'Dart', possibly meaning 'oak'. **DARTMOOR'S NAMES** feature hills, tors, rivers and particular places. These include some weird and wonderful names. Most of these keep the secrets of their name origins to themselves, which may be just as well in some cases! Here are just some of them; Bot Tor, Bughead Cross, Click Tor, Cowsic River, Chilly Wood, Deadman's Bottom, Dick's Well, Dinger Tor, Evil Combe, Fitz's Well, Fritz's Grave, Gobbet Plain, Golden Dagger Mine, Goodlay's Plantation, Gutter Mire, Herring's Knock, Honeybag Tor, Hooten Wheals, Horseyeat, Kiss-in-the-Ring, Klondyke Corner, Knackersmill Gulf, The Lick, Look-and-Weep, Lucky Tor, Mistress Piece, Mucks Hole Bridge, Naked Hill, Nipper's Hole, Nutcrackers, Pixies Parlour, Plague Market, Princep's Folly, Puggie Stone, Rogues Roost, Shovel Down, Slipper Stones, Stinka Tor, Stumpy Cross, Urgles, Whooping

Rock, Whisky and Soda Wood (make mine a double!), Woolholes, and Witz End, which is probably where you are at right now! (See also **UNUSUAL NAMES.**)

DARTMOUTH is at, or very close to, the mouth of the Dart.

DAWLISH means 'black water' or 'Devil water' and is one of the oldest local names. The stream, so much a part of the resort, is simply called 'The Brook' and not the River Daw as some guide books have called it in the past. There have been no less than 30 variations in the spelling.

DAWLISH WARREN is a name created by the Great Western Railway, who developed a railway halt close to the Warren sand spit. This feature is well over a mile in length and one which funnels the mouth of the Exe estuary. Prior to that it was often referred to as 'Exmouth Warren' as the distal end was closer to this resort than Dawlish. Once there was a weird assortment of holiday homes on the Warren's tip, and summer residents usually opted to get their provisions from Exmouth rather than from the shop at the Dawlish end of the spit. These Bohemian-styled dwellings were largely washed away during storms in the 1920s and '30s. None survive! However, the 'business end' of Dawlish Warren has grown appreciably in recent decades.

DEAN PRIOR, near Buckfastleigh, takes its name from the endowments of the wealthy Priory of Plympton, to which it was given by William Fitz Stephen in the reign of Henry II.

DENBURY is an ancient place, once called 'Devenabury', dominated by the prominent hill of the same name. It means 'the fort of the men of Devon'.

DEVIL occurs in Devil's Point, Plymouth, and also at Devil's Tor and Devil's Elbow on Dartmoor. The latter was a particularly sharp bend near Princetown which has been straightened out. It lent its name to a pub in Princetown, but in recent years this has been changed to the Railway Inn. As true Devonians will tell you, the Devil lives in Devon.

DEVON or **DEVONSHIRE?** That's the question I have often faced when deciding on book titles but in most cases (with the exception of *Diary of a Devonshire Walker*) I have plumped for the shorter form of the name. The Anglo-Saxons called the area as far west as the Tamar, the county border with Cornwall, 'Defnascir'. The first part of the name means 'the men of Devon' and the second part means 'shire'. Down the years this has corrupted to Devonshire.

DEVONPORT was originally known as Plymouth Dock, but most folks simply called it 'Dock'. It became Devonport in 1824: no longer the 'Dock of Plymouth' but the 'Port of Devon'!

DIPTFORD is on the hill above the River Avon. Its name means 'deep ford', which seems to be a contradiction in terms as most people would expect to cross where it's shallow!

DITTISHAM, pronounced 'Ditsum', is the farm named after 'Dyddi' who 'did die' long ago! This is a riverside village on the Dart estuary.

DODDISCOMBSLEIGH with 16 letters is something of a mouthful. A lot of locals shorten it down, in conversation, to the friendly-sounding 'Doddi'. It means something like 'the clearing of the Doddescombe family', who held the land from about 1260.

DRAKE'S ISLAND is in Plymouth Sound just off Plymouth Hoe. The island's original name was St Michael's, after a church of that dedication built on it. The state later assumed control, for defence purposes, and rechristened it St Nicholas Island; but some 150 years after the death of Sir Francis Drake he was honoured when it was renamed, for a third time, 'Drake's Island'.

DRANG, a dialect term, means an alleyway or passageway. Few places have it as a specific name but there are examples like Emberry's Drang in Bideford.

DREWSTEIGNTON comes from the personal name of Dru or Drogo who settled a farm on the hills close to the River Teign. Castle Drogo, on the edge of the moor is sometimes billed as 'the newest castle in England', a National Trust property previously owned by the Drewe family. Julius Drewe had it built between 1910 and 1930 on land acquired from the church. He chose a spot where he believed his ancestors lived, probably in the early thirteenth century, and the celebrated Sir Edwin Lutyens was the architect of this fine building.

DUMPDON HILL, a hill fort near Honiton in the Otter valley, means 'circular hill'.

DUNCHIDEOCK, pronounced without sounding the 'e', means 'the wooded fort', this probably being the one at nearby Cotley, in the hills above this village.

DUNKESWELL, once the site of an important Cistercian abbey, is often misspelt with an 'r' inserted between the 'e' and the 's'. Its interpretation is open to debate. One attempt links it to the Dunnock or hedge-sparrow. Another is 'the well of dark water', which seems more likely.

DUNSFORD lies on the edge of Dartmoor, close to the banks of the River Teign, which could be forded here. 'Dun' in a place-name usually means a flat-topped hill or ridge, but here it's believed to mean 'cattle ford' or, more simply, 'Dunn's ford'.

DUNTERTON, high above the Tamar valley, possibly means 'fort farm'.

DUNSTONE is a hamlet near Widecombe and means 'by the grey rock'. It is still there, a reminder of the times when dues which were owed were paid here, probably on one occasion each year. The 'Dun Stone' has also been called the 'Rent Stone' for this reason.

EAST ALLINGTON, 'Aetha's land', is in the heart of the South Hams country.

EAST BUDLEIGH is derived from 'Budda's leigh' or a clearing formed by him.

EAST OGWELL, near Newton Abbot, is where 'Wogga's spring' was located.

EAST PORTLEMOUTH, opposite Salcombe, used to be the more important. This is reflected in its place-name which means 'the landing place at the mouth of the estuary'.

EFFORD, in Plymouth, probably derives from 'ebb-ford'.

EGGESFORD, where for many years the population was 88, is from 'Ecgen's ford'.

ELBURTON, on the outskirts of Plymouth, is a corruption of Aliburton which it was in 1254. The first part of the name probably refers to the Saxon who founded the settlement.

ELEPHANT'S NEST is the unusual name of a pub at Horndon, a hamlet near Mary Tavy. Originally the New Inn, it had a landlord of incredible bulk, who sat on a stool and did as much serving as he could without leaving it, and regulars reckoned he looked like an elephant sat on a nest. This notion appealed to him so much that he changed the name of the pub, this happening sometime in the 1950s. The Elephant has since flown the nest!

EPHRAIM'S PINCH is a hill within Soussons Down plantation on Dartmoor. It is reputedly named after poor Ephraim, who had to prove his strength, to his would-be father-in-law, by carrying a heavy sack over a long distance. This is where he collapsed and died. A harsh trial!

ERNESETTLE in Plymouth, has a similar meaning to Yes Tor on Dartmoor, which was once called Ernestorre. Both mean 'eagles' hill'.

ERMINGTON is 'the farm by the River Erme' and, unusually, it is this village which gives its name to the river, a good example of a back formation.

EXE, like Axe, means 'water'.

EXETER is a Cathedral city and the county town. The ancient British name was Caerwysc – 'the fortified town on the Exe'. When the Romans arrived it was 'Caer-pen-huel-goit', which meant something like 'the fortified place, on the hill, in or near the great wood'. The Romans named the settlement 'Isca Dumnoniorum', after 'the camp of the Dumnonii tribe' who had settled here centuries earlier. By the year 750 it was called Exanceaster, in 1050 Execester, and in 1547 Exeter. There were several variations in between.

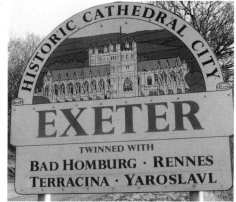

EXMINSTER is 'the church (of St Martin) beside the Exe' but it's a bit of a walk to the river. The village, which has mushroomed in recent years, has grown up on the edge of the wide flood plain. The local soccer team take their name from the church.

EXMOUTH, as you would guess, is at 'the mouth of the Exe'.

FAIRMILE, between Exeter and Honiton, lies on the route of a Roman road. It has been suggested that nearby was a good stretch of road, rare in muddy Devon, a 'fair mile'. The hill towards Exeter rises for about a mile. Road protesters put the name on the map in 1996. With the arrival of the new route for the A30 the dangerous dip at Fairmile is 'by-passed'.

FARRINGDON probably means 'bracken hill'.

FARWAY, in East Devon, probably takes its name from a nearby road which follows an ancient ridgeway, as does the present highway between Ottery St Mary and Seaton, 'the faer-weg' meaning 'the frequented road'.

FENITON, near Honiton, is 'a farm near the fen or marsh by the bridge' over the Otter. The old village, centred on its lovely church, is well away from the modern dormitory settlement.

FERRERS is a common appendage to some 30 place names throughout the country. In Devon it follows Newton, Churston and Bere. It derives from a French family who supported William the Conqueror and who were well rewarded for their efforts. They originated in NW France and were the owners of the biggest iron mines in that part of the world.

FILLEIGH means 'a hay clearing' or may take its name from the church, dedicated to St Fili.

FINGLE BRIDGE spans the Teign near Drewsteignton. It's a fine river for fishing and Fingle is believed to mean something like 'a place where a good catch could be expected'.

FORCHES, as a place-name, is probably more common than you might imagine and derives from a French word meaning a place where executions by hanging from the gallows took place, this often being on the edge of a parish. The pub at Clyst Hydon is called the Forches Cross Inn.

FREMINGTON, between Barnstaple and Bideford, was known as Framintona in 1086. 'Freming' is the corruption of a personal name.

GALMPTON, of which there are two in Devon, one near Hope Cove and the other on the Dart near Churston Ferrers, possibly means 'a farm run by rent-paying peasants'.

GAPPAH, near Chudleigh, means 'goats' path' and was a hillside route.

GEORGEHAM was originally just called 'Ham'. The church is dedicated to St George.

GEORGENYMPTON is the first place, alphabetically, to have Nympton as part of its name. There are many others. 'Nympton' derives from the word 'Nemeton' meaning a holy place or grove where worship took place, probably before churches were built. To differentiate from the others this one is named after the church of St George. (See also **NYMET**.)

GERMANSWEEK is small and in West Devon. The 'week' part derives from 'wick', meaning 'dairy farm'. The dedication of the village church is to St Germanus of Auxerre.

GIBBET HILL is high above Lydford and on the western side of Dartmoor. It was aptly named for many executions took place here. There was a rhyme, by William Browne, which varies in the reciting, that says something like "Have you heard of Lydford law, Where in the morn they hang and draw, And sit in judgment after." This is where they performed the gruesome tasks.

GIDLEIGH, about three miles from Chagford, is probably 'Gydda's clearing in the forest'.

GISSAGE is a steeply profiled stream which joins the Otter. It has caused flooding in Honiton. Its name gives a hint of the menace because it probably means 'a strong or gushing flow'.

GITTISHAM is pronounced 'Gitsum'. The stream here is charmingly named 'River Git'. This village in East Devon is named after Gyddi.

GLAZE BROOK is a tributary of the Avon. Its name may mean 'grey brook'.

GOODRINGTON, a part of Paignton, was probably 'Godhere's farm'.

GOYLE is a common name in East Devon, and means a deep, steep-sided valley.

GREAT TORRINGTON was, of old, Cheping Torrington. The word 'Cheping' means 'market'. As there were so many places called 'Torrington' a prefix was added to differentiate from the others. It is a hill-top village and means 'the farm by the river Torridge'.

GREENLAND LAKE was once an inlet in the great sandspit of Dawlish Warren. It ceased to exist as a tidal channel when it was dammed and drained. It's believed that fishing boats, which used to go to the Greenland fisheries, sheltered here in times of storm when in home waters.

GRINDLE BROOK, 'the gravelly brook', is a tributary of the Clyst.

GULWORTHY, a small hamlet near Tavistock, and on a high hill above the Tamar Valley, was once important for its abbey and it's possible that its name means 'Abbot's weir'.

HALBERTON, on the banks of the Tiverton or Grand Western Canal, was named Halsbreton in 1086. Possibly it has arrived at today's name from 'Haligbeorht's farm'.

HALDON is an elevated escarpment which forms a watershed between the lower Exe and middle Teign valleys. It may mean 'look-out hill', 'high hill', 'hill of hail' or even 'holy hill'.

HALWELL, between Totnes and Kingsbridge, means 'holy well' which, like Halwill, if said in a lazy, slurred fashion, will sound like today's place-name!

HALWILL, once a railway junction of importance, and in 'the middle of nowhere', also takes its name from the presence of a 'holy well'.

HAMEL DOWN is a great humped-back hill. It possibly means 'cut-off hill' and it certainly stands 'head and shoulders' above the surrounding hills and tors.

HAMOAZE is a strange name. It is used today for the part of the Tamar near its mouth. It probably means 'the manor close to the shallow muddy creek'. This would probably have referred to one of the Tamar's inlets as it is now very deep where the Hamoaze is shown on the map.

HARBERTON, along with Harbertonford and Harbourneford, takes its name from the River Harbourne, which flows into the Dart's estuary. The old name for Harbertonford was Hernaford.

HARBOURNE, as above, may mean either 'deer stream' or 'gentle stream'.

HARCOMBE, on the western side of Haldon, near Chudleigh, is 'hare valley'.

HARFORD shares with the military town of Hereford a place-name of which the first part means 'army'. However, as other eminent historians have noted, the history behind this is not known. Any 'ford' would have been over the nearby, and very beautiful, River Erme.

HARPFORD derives from its location close to where an ancient routeway, the 'harepath', crossed the River Otter.

HARROWBEER appears a few times in Devon and means 'the wood of the hares'.

HARTLAND, despite being part of mainland North Devon, means 'stag-island'.

HATHERLEIGH, a market town of real character six miles from Okehampton, means either 'a clearing in the hawthorn wood' or 'heath land' or 'heather'. Above the town is the open space of Hatherleigh Moor.

HAWKCHURCH used to be in Dorset but now it's 'come home' to Devon! The first part is derived from a personal name, possibly 'Hafoc'.

HAY, which means 'an area of enclosed ground', occurs in many place-names, particularly in East Devon and in Exeter. In the county town examples include Friernhay, Bonhay, Southernhay, Northernhay and Shilhay. Some of these were areas where the processing of wool took place.

HAYNE means, more or less, the same as 'hay' and is also common in East Devon.

HEANTON PUNCHARDON, near Barnstaple, with two distinctly different parts to its name, sounds more like a Dorset place-name. The first part means 'high farm'. Sir Robert de Punchardon came over with William the Conqueror and was given this land as his reward.

HEAVITREE, now a part of Exeter, was, until 1913, a separate settlement. There has been much debate about the origin of this place-name. It is believed that it's derived from an important tree, possibly 'Hefa's tree', named after the tribal chief. The name is well known across the region because of the celebrated and long-established brewery of this name. Although it no longer brews its own beers it still oversees more than a hundred pubs, 'Heavitree Houses', in the South-West.

HEMERDON, on the edge of Dartmoor, possibly means 'the hill by the hen pool'.

HEMYOCK, in the Culm Valley, means the 'ever-flowing stream'.

HENNOCK, high above the Teign valley, possibly means 'tall or high oak'.

HIGHAMPTON, from its elevated position, overlooks Northern Dartmoor.

HOE is either 'a high place' or 'a projecting ridge of land'. In the case of Plymouth Hoe, a famous name the world over, it is the former, a limestone hill of great significance.

HOLBETON, close to the mouth of the River Erme, is 'the farm in a hollow and on a bend'.

HOLCOMBE, between Dawlish and Teignmouth, means 'hollow valley'.

HOLCOMBE ROGUS is another 'hollow valley'. It was once owned by Rogo, whose son, Simon, gave Holcombe's church to the priory at Montacute, in Somerset, about 1156. Jordan Roges held the manor in 1238.

HOLLACOMBE is a common place-name in Devon and means 'hollow valley'.

HOLNE, on Dartmoor, is 'the place where the holly thrives'.

HOLSWORTHY, miles from the sea, became a 'Port Town' a millennium ago, this being an enclosed and safe 'harbourage' for travellers and their various chattels. It is derived from 'Harold's Worthy' after the King killed at the Battle of Hastings in 1066, who owned land here.

HONICKNOWLE, in Plymouth, means 'Hana's Hill'.

HONITON, in the Otter valley, is most likely to be derived from 'Huna's farm'.

HORNDON is 'a hill above the bend of a river', this being the Tavy.

HORRABRIDGE is both the name of the village and its ancient, fourteenth century three-arched span over the River Walkham, a tributary of the Tavy. One suggestion is that it means 'the bridge from where the hares may be sighted', a tie-in with neighbouring Harrowbeer, featured earlier.

HORSE BRIDGE spans the Tamar above Gunnislake. Its name has nothing to do with four-legged friends. It comes from 'Hautes' meaning 'high bridge'.

HORWOOD may mean 'grey wood' or 'muddy wood'.

HUCCABY is a hamlet and a bridge over the West Dart near Dartmeet. It is also often called Hexworthy. Here the river begins a big loop and it is this from which the place derives its name.

HUISH, commonly found across the region, is 'land owned by one household'.

HUNTSHAW means 'honey wood' which may give some folks a bit of a buzz!

IDE is a small village on the south-western outskirts of Exeter. Its name is pronounced to rhyme with 'weed' and not 'died'. The village name is believed to have been derived from the church of St Ida, dedicated to a German saint. Coincidentally there is a fish called an Ide which grows to about a metre in length and is found in lakes in Bavaria, Germany! Many Americans bear the surname Ide and the village seems to draw them like a magnet.

ILFRACOMBE, the largest resort in North Devon, means 'Aelfred's valley' and may be, somewhat romantically, named after Alfred the Great.

ILSHAM, in Torquay, could mean 'the home of hedgehogs',

INSTOW, opposite Appledore at the mouth of the Torridge, is a corruption of 'Yonestowe' or 'Jonestow' which is 'the shrine of St John'. In 1260 it was recorded as St Johanues Stow.

INWARDLEIGH comes from its Domesday owner, one Inwar.

IPPLEPEN is a long village, between Newton Abbot and Totnes, which has grown in recent years. In 956 it was Iplanpen. Its name possibly has a first part from the settlement founder. 'Pen' oftens means a hill when used in a place-name, as in Pennsylvania (the wooded hill) in Exeter.

ISAAC MERRITT is the name of a pub at Paignton which honours Mr Singer, the man who mass-produced the sewing machine. He moved from Paris to Paignton and was a kindly man, often treating all the children of the town to sweets. His wife is believed to have been the model who Bartholdi used for the crowning-glory of the Statue of Liberty in New York.

IVYBRIDGE takes its name from the ancient, single-arched Ivy Bridge over the River Erme, a bridge where four parish bounds join.

JACOBSTOWE is the sole village name in Devon to start with a 'J'. There is another 'Jacobstow', minus an 'e', in Cornwall. Its name derives from its most 'holy' feature, the church of St James, also known as St Jacob.

JOURNEY'S END is the name of a lovely pub at Ringmore, the one not far from from Modbury. Its name is derived from a play of the same name which was written by R. C. Sheriff. First staged in 1929, it received the accolade of 'the most wonderful play ever written'!

KATE BROOK, 'the heron pool stream', flows below Chudleigh into the Teign.

KELLY, now a popular Christian name for girls, occurs in parts of many place-names in Devon. In most cases it means 'grove', but in the single-named village it is after a mediaeval family.

KELLY COLLEGE, at Tavistock, takes its name from Admiral Benedictus Marwood Kelly, native of Hatherleigh, who posthumously funded, on a site given by the Duke of Bedford, a school 'for the sons of naval officers and other gentlemen'.

KENN, as in the river of that name, means 'brilliant or white'. It joins the Exe at Powderham. There is also a village called Kenn beside this stream, and the same situation is also found in Somerset with village and river juxtaposed.

KENNERLEIGH is probably 'Cyneweard's clearing'.

KENTISBEARE, in East Devon and on the small River Ken, possibly means 'Centa's wood'.

KENTISBURY is from a nearby 'earthwork on the rounded hill'.

KENTON is the 'farm by the river Kenn'.

KINGSBRIDGE is the 'Capital of the South Hams' where, in the tenth century, there was a bridge linking two royal estates, those of Alvington and Chillington: thus it was 'King's Bridge'. Many towns in Devon have had a variety of spellings (Dawlish, Paignton and Cullompton all having 30 or more each!) and it would be tedious to deal with every variation for each place, but just so that you will get the picture, here are some of those for Kingsbridge: **Kynggesbrigge, Kyngesbrygge, Kyngisbrugge, Kynsbrygge, Kingisbrigge, Kynesbrugge, Kyngesbrigge, Kyngysbryghe** and so it goes on with almost any permutation of the same letters. The other part of the town is Dodbrooke which was 'Dodda's brook'.

KINGSKERSWELL is 'the spring on the King's land where water-cress grows'.

KINGSTEIGNTON, held by the King in 1086, is supposedly one of the biggest, but not prettiest, villages in England. It's 'the King's farm by the Teign'.

KINGSTON is 'the King's farm', but which monarch remains a mystery.

KINGSWEAR is 'the King's weir', an unknown king of pre-Norman times.

KISMELDON BRIDGE over the River Torridge derives its name from 'cristelmael' which means crucifix.

KNOWSTONE, pronounced 'now-stone', may be from Cnutsan or Cnut.

LAIRA, Plymouth, occupies land reclaimed from a tidal inlet off the Plym estuary. This was once known as Leeri or Lary and is derived from another Saxon word meaning 'to ebb or grow shallow'. Some interpret it to mean 'lesser water'.

LAKE on Dartmoor is often found in stream names, e.g. Dead Lake, Red Lake, Dark Lake.

LAMERTON, near Tavistock, is believed to mean 'the lambs' grazing place near the river'.

LANDKEY, in North Devon, is named after the church of St Cai, a Celtic saint.

LAPFORD may take its name from a person, or it may derive from a point on the river where 'a ford marked by leaps' enabled fish to be caught.

Place-Names in Devon

LEMON is a lively river which rises near Haytor to join the Teign at Newton Abbot. Its name means 'elm bordered'. Lemonford is a hamlet in its upper reaches.

LETTAFORD, near Chagford, contains a fine example of a Dartmoor longhouse. Its name is believed to mean 'the ford over the clear stream'.

LEWTRENCHARD on the Lew ('bright stream') is where the Trenchard family were in 1238.

LINCOMBE, as found in Torquay, means 'the valley of the clear-running stream'.

LITTLE SILVER is a common name in Devon, with examples found in the parishes of Romansleigh, Shobrooke, Marwood, High Bickington, Great Torrington, Cadeleigh, Tiverton, and Clyst Honiton. Despite this there is no proven interpretation for the meaning of this frequent name. It is unlikely to come from the precious metal as it's not found in most of these places. It's possible that it might refer to the small, shining streams that flow through these settlements.

LODDISWELL, from 'Lodd's spring', is high on a hill above the river Avon.

LOXHORE, in North Devon, has evolved from its Saxon name of 'Locca's Bank'.

LUFFINCOTT, above the Tamar, was probably 'the cot of Luhha's people'.

LUNDY means 'Puffin Isle', and this bird has been adopted as the symbol for Lundy currency and frequently appears on the island's own stamps. The puffin is known as 'the Lundy parrot'.

LUPPITT, on the edge of the Blackdown Hills near Honiton, is probably 'Lufa's hollow or pit'. Although many miles from the sea, like Wigan Pier, many people refer to 'Luppitt Harbour'.

LUSTLEIGH, lovely village of Eastern Dartmoor, is possibly 'the forest clearing of Luvesta'. 'Lust', or any other deadly sin, is not involved for 'Luvesta' is supposed to mean 'dearest one'.

LYDFORD is one of the four ancient boroughs of Devon, a 'town' that suddenly stopped growing whilst some of its neighbours assumed greater importance. However, it is still the biggest parish in England even though the great majority of it is open, wild and remote moorland. It is located on the river Lyd, which means 'loud or noisy stream' where, no doubt, it could easily be forded.

LYMPSTONE is an almost impossible name to interpret. Whether or not its name of 1434, which was Limestone, is a clue to its meaning isn't known.

LYNTON and **LYNMOUTH** are two villages in North Devon, the former high on a hill above the rivers East and West Lyn which join forces here before plunging into the sea. These rivers, aided by the flows of a number of smaller streams caused immense destruction and carnage at Lynmouth in August 1952 when 31 people lost their lives in the flood. 'Lyn' means 'torrent stream'!

MAIDENCOMBE is between Torquay and Teignmouth and was, at one time, called 'Minicombe' meaning 'small valley'. Its present name means 'the valley of maidens'.

MALBOROUGH, in the South Hams, means 'Maerla's fortified hill'.

MAMHEAD, on the edge of Haldon, means a 'hill the shape of a teat'.

MANGA HILL and Manga Falls, on the North Teign river on Dartmoor, derive their names from a Gaelic word which means 'a boundary mark'.

MARISTOW, on the Tavy's estuary, was Martinstowe, 'Martin's holy place', after a chapel dedicated to St Martin de Blakestane. Blaxton, a corrupted name, is nearby!

MARLDON, near Paignton, should be 'the hill of marl' but it isn't! It is 'the hill where the meargealle grew'. This old English word is for a plant called Gentian. In 1949 Elizabeth Gouge, who lived here, published her novel *Gentian Hill,* which was set in this area. She had already written *Smoky House,* the name of a pub at Marldon.

MARTINHOE in North Devon is 'the high place' or ridge location of the founder's settlement.

MARWOOD, in North Devon, is believed to mean 'boundary wood'.

MARYSTOW, just to the NW of Dartmoor, is 'the holy place of St Mary'.

MARY TAVY is named after the Church of St Mary in the Tavy valley.

MATFORD is on the outskirts of Exeter and possibly means 'maidens' ford'.

MEAVY or Mewy derives from an old Devonshire word for a seagull. However, some say it means 'merry river' and others 'loud river' or 'greater water'.

MEETH possibly means 'hay land'.

MEMBURY, in East Devon, takes its name from an ancient hill fort and means 'stone castle'.

MERRIPIT HILL is the big hill, haunted by ghostly pigs, above Postbridge. Its name refers to its lower slopes because it means 'pleasant hollow'.

MERRIVALE, a Dartmoor hamlet on the River Walkham, might possibly mean 'the pleasant tree-free open space'. Certainly nothing much grows above Merrivale Bridge.

MERTON, 'farm by the River Mere', is not named after a comedian!

MESHAW, near South Molton, may mean 'infertile clearing'.

MEW STONE is a common name around the coasts of Devon and means 'a rock inhabited by seagulls'. The Great Mew Stone near Plymouth is a good example.

MILLBAY, as in Plymouth, is where there was once a tidal mill.

MILTON ABBOT, where the 'mill farm of the abbots' existed, was once owned by Tavistock Abbey. However, others believe that it was 'the middle land between Lamerton and Dunterton'.

MILTON COMBE, near Roborough Down, may mean 'middle farm in the valley'.

MINCINGLAKE is a road in Exeter which derives its name from a stream, now largely in culverts. It means 'Nun's stream' and derives from a former nunnery once on its banks.

MODBURY is believed to mean 'moot hill'. Moot, in Anglo-Saxon England, was an assembly dealing with local administrative or legal matters.

MOLLAND, on the edge of Exmoor, is where I gave my first talk to a WI group! It was known as 'Molland Bottreaux' at one time. It came to the Bottreaux family after the Norman Conquest.

MONKERTON is now part of an expanding Pinhoe, on the edge of Exeter. A housing estate now occupies 'the virgate of land held by the monks of Battle Abbey'.

MONKLEIGH was granted to the monks of Montacute in Somerset.

MONKOKEHAMPTON, three miles from Hatherleigh, means 'an enclosed farm, of the monks, there before the eleventh century, on the River Ockment or Okement'.

MONKTON, near Honiton, means 'monks' farm', probably from Anglo-Saxon times.

MORCHARD BISHOP is the 'great wood', possibly of a bishop.

MOREBATH, near Dulverton, is where chalybeate springs, containing iron salts, are found.

MORETONHAMPSTEAD is 'more' or less self-explanatory – 'moorland farm homestead'. However the first part of the name could well mean 'marshy land'.

MORTEHOE may mean 'death hill', and takes its name from nearby Morte Point. A local saying states 'Morte is the place which Heaven made last and the Devil will take first!'

MORWELLHAM is an ancient river port on the Tamar and now a major tourist attraction, a living museum to reflect the valley's mining and trading past. It means something like 'the flat fenland beside the stream' and that is a fair reflection of its site.

MOTHECOMBE, at the mouth of the Erme, means 'the mouth of the valley'.

MOUNT BATTEN, at Plymouth, harks back to the Civil War (1642–1646) when Admiral Batten admirably defended his fort, which was under siege.

MOUNT GOULD, also in Plymouth, was similarly named in honour of Colonel Gould, who also stoutly refused to give in to the Royalist attackers and who was responsible for building up much of the town's defences. He led the troops in the famous victory known as the 'Sabbath Day Fight', now commemorated by a memorial in the aptly-named 'Freedom Fields'. Plymouth boasts many names of streets and features which reflect this prolonged assault on the city.

MUSBURY, unlikely as it may seem, may mean 'fort of mice'. In Old English 'mus' was mouse so this East Devon village's fort may have once been infested.

MUTLEY, in Plymouth, may not be a 'dastardly' place, but a precise translation is not forthcoming.

NADDERWATER is a hamlet on the western side of Exeter, just a short way outside the city limits. Its name has a Celtic origin and it has evolved from its stream, the Nadder Brook, which was "Nywdd-dwr" meaning 'the stronger flowing water'. There is no doubt that this steeply-profiled stream has been known to cause floods lower down its course. In October 1960, having added its flow to the Alphin Brook, it helped to swamp the nether regions of Exeter. One local who approached me whilst I took this picture, in the absence of a village sign, told me that 'Nobody knew where the disseminated hamlet of Nadderwater started or finished!'

NETHEREXE is a hamlet in the Exe Valley. It is low-lying (nether) and beside the Exe. It's possible that it could mean that it was lower down the valley than nearby Up Exe.

NETHERTON, on the banks of the Teign estuary, means 'lower farm'.

NEWTON ABBOT is the 'new town of the Abbots' of Torre Abbey. They were, no doubt, pleased to receive the land in 1196 from William de Briwere.

NEWTON FERRERS (see **FERRERS**) is 'the new farm of the Ferrers family'. Although this is a small Devon village the Newton Ferrers in East Cornwall is smaller still!

NEWTON POPPLEFORD is the 'new farm by the pebble ford'.

NEWTON ST CYRES has a splendid church, that of St Julitta and St Cyriac.

NEWTON ST PETROCK has the church of St Petrock, a fourteenth or fifteenth century structure, to thank for its name. In 938 it was granted by King Athelstan to St Petrock's monastery at Bodmin.

NEWTON TRACEY was the 'new farm of Henry de Tracey', who held the manor in 1282.

NOBODY INN, the village pub at Doddiscombsleigh, was originally the New Inn. It changed in the mid-1950s after the death, in 1952, of Dick Lewis, the landlord. Apparently he had 'wasted away to nothing' and his coffin was mistakenly buried in the churchyard with 'no body in' it! The next landlord thought it a bit of a joke and changed the pub's name to what it still is to this day.

NORTHLEW is where the Devil supposedly died from the cold! It is on a hill above the River Lew. The 'North' differentiates it from Lewtrenchard, once simply referred to as 'Lew'.

NORTH MOLTON lies in the valley of the River Mole which provides an example of a back formation, the river deriving its name from the Molton. It's farther north than South Molton.

NORTH TAWTON was, at the time of Domesday, Tawetona or Tawland, this referring to its position by the River Taw. In 1199 it was called 'Cheping Tawton'. However it was possibly laziness which led to the dropping of the first part of its name. Possibly to differentiate it from its counterpart, South Tawton, a 'North' was added. Too many Tawtons could be confusing!

NOSS MAYO, opposite Newton Ferrers, is believed to derive from a combination of an Old English word meaning 'headland or promontory' followed by a personal name. Mayo, common in Ireland, is a variant of Matthew, this time Mathew Johannis who once held the manor.

NYMET has the same meaning as 'Newtake', a word found on Dartmoor to account for enclosures of moorland to be reclaimed from wasteland. Examples include Nymet Rowland.

OAKFORD is self-explanatory so I won't explain it!

OFFWELL was 'Offa's Well'.

OKEHAMPTON is the 'farm by the Okement' and the two courses, East and West Okement, which flow off the high northern moors of Dartmoor, unite in the town. The 'oke' part is from the Old English spelling for oak.

OPE is short for opening and is found in many Plymouth street names, particularly in the Barbican and Stonehouse, waterside areas of the city, where Basket Ope and Admiralty Ope are examples.

OTTERTON, a beautiful village in East Devon, is 'the farm by the Otter'.

OTTERY ST MARY is in the Otter valley. The wonderful church of St Mary is often referred to as 'the Cathedral of East Devon' because it is regarded as a smaller version of Exeter Cathedral.

PACK OF CARDS is a most unusually designed pub in Combe Martin. It is aptly named as it has four floors to match the four suits, thirteen doors on each floor to match the cards in a suit, 52 windows to equal the number in a pack. It's also 52 feet square and 52 feet tall! It was the brainchild of local squire George Ley, who was an inveterate gambler.

PAIGNTON is 'Paga's farm', once an agricultural settlement of great importance, now a bustling and boisterous seaside resort. It has endured many spellings. There are still milestones around which bear the once-preferred version of 'Paington'.

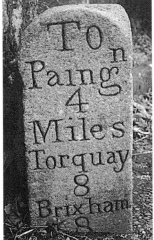

PANCRASWEEK, like Germansweek, is a combination of saint and farm but this time it's St Pancras, who has stolen the limelight.

PARKHAM, in North Devon, is perhaps 'the farm with small enclosures'.

PARRACOMBE on Exmoor possibly derives from 'the pedlar's valley'.

PAYHEMBURY is near Hembury hill fort. An early landowner was 'Paie'.

PENNYCOMEQUICK, found in the name of a district of Plymouth, and also in Cornwall, is believed to be Celtic and may well derive from 'pen y cwm cuig', 'where the creek meets the end of a valley', the word 'cuig' being 'creek'. In Wales there are many 'Penycwms'.

PETERS MARLAND, near Hatherleigh, has the church of St Peter and is near the River Mere which flows through commercial clay-producing country.

PETER TAVY is named after the Church of St Peter near the River Tavy.

PETROCKSTOW is 'the holy place of St Petrock', a saint well represented in Devon. He must have had a good publicity agent!

PILLS are not just tablets! In many parts of Devon where there are estuaries it is quite common to find the word 'Pill' used as a common noun or even as a name for a tidal inlet, muddy at low water, like a lake at high tide. Pillmouth is a hamlet where such an inlet joins the Torridge estuary, near Bideford. Many have been reclaimed, so the expression 'Keep taking the pills' might be more ambiguous than you imagine!

PINHOE is a superb suburb of Exeter. The church is high above the village, possibly the 'hoe' or high place. 'Pin', in this instance, may be like 'pen', meaning a hill.

PLYMOUTH is Devon's largest settlement and has spread from the mouth of the Plym, hence its name, across to the more navigable and important Tamar.

PLYMSTOCK is possibly the 'place where the plum trees grow'. However, 'stock' in this case may mean an 'outlying settlement'.

PLYMTREE is not on the River Plym! It is a small village in East Devon, about three miles from Cullompton, and possibly also derives from 'plum tree'.

POLSLOE is a part of Exeter. It possibly means 'Pol's marsh'.

POLTIMORE, near Exeter, is a village without a pub! The first part of the name, 'pol', is common in Cornwall and means 'pool'. The possible translation of the whole name is 'on marshy ground near the river'. In this case it would be the River Clyst, now flowing just beyond by the M5, which runs between it and the village. Poltimore Park is low-lying and after heavy rain floods.

POUGHILL, 'Pohha's hill', is pronounced 'poil' to rhyme with 'boil'!

POWDERHAM, just like the Dutch 'polder', is 'a farm on reclaimed land'. Kenton was once a port, on a tidal inlet, but the River Kenn's estuary, at Powderham, has been drained and now there is little sign of the former creek apart from occasions when floods arise.

PRAWLE POINT, which some authorities say means 'look-out hill', is the most southerly headland in Devon. Early in the twentieth century it was the location of a Lloyd's Signal Station; the building, now derelict, still sits on this rocky eminence. Others favour the meaning as 'skull' from the Celtic 'pral', on account of dark deeds done here in the past …

PRINCETOWN was the 'brainwave' of Sir Thomas Tyrwhitt, friend of the Prince of Wales, later George IV, who 'had a dream'. He wanted to tame the wild moors of upland Dartmoor and to

PRINCETOWN
Please drive slowly

transform them into a productive agricultural area. This was not to be; but after defeat he 'struck lucky' in the building here of a 'war depot' to house French, and later American, prisoners of war. His settlement of Prince's Town was named after the Prince of Wales, whose coat of arms is seen in this windswept, rain-lashed upland village.

PUDDINGTON where 'Jan Stewer' (A. J. Coles), a master of Devon dialect stories, once taught, was 'Putta's farm'.

QUEENS NYMPTON, an outlying district of South Molton, is our only 'Q'. It is a relatively new name which goes back to 1900 when Queen Victoria was honoured.

RACKENFORD, in mid-Devon, may well mean 'houses by the path leading to the ford'.

RATTERY, near Buckfastleigh, probably means 'at the red tree'. Certainly the village sign reflects this explanation for the place-name.

RATTLEBROOK, a tributary of the Tavy, means 'rash or hasty stream', which it often is!

RAWRIDGE, which means 'rough hill', is between Honiton and Upottery.

RING-IN-THE-MIRE is the swampy place, near the Hare & Hounds pub on Gittisham Hill, where the parishes of Honiton, Farway, Gittisham and Sidbury meet. The Countess of Devon, Isabella de Fortibus, is reputed to have summoned a meeting here of representatives of three of these parishes who disputed the boundaries. In their presence she took off a ring and tossed it into the mire, saying that where the ring fell was the meeting place of these parishes. However, although it's a nice story it's more likely that the name is much older.

RINGMORE is found in the name of two villages in South Devon, one on the Teign estuary, an extension of Shaldon, and the other deep in the South Hams, near Bigbury-on-Sea. The latter is possibly derived from the Celtic 'rhyn-mawr' which means 'the great headland'.

RIVER NAMES mostly derive, not surprisingly, from a very damp source! R. N. Worth wrote this in his *History of Devonshire*, first published in 1907: *"All the larger rivers have Keltic names; so have those in the middle class; and it is only when we come to the smaller streams that the Saxon can be traced. Minor affluents had no distinctive name in early Keltic times, nor would they receive any until the county was more thickly populated. The most remarkable river group is that which contains the Tamar, Tavy, Taw, Torridge and Teign – all questionably related and all based upon one root word for water, ta or tau, with varying suffixes for the purposes of definition. Thus Tamar is Ta-maur, the 'big water;' Tavy, Ta-vean, the 'little water.' In the Exe and the Axe we have the Gaelic uisg, again 'water'; and in Avon, afon, one of the commonest Kymric words for a river. Dart is the same name as Derwent, derivable from the old Kornu-Keltic Dwr-gwyn, the 'white river' or water. Dwr also appears in the Derle and the Deer, and probably in Otter, as ydwr = 'the water'. These are merely suggestive hints … A few Saxon names may, however, be mentioned. Lyn= hlynn a 'stream.' In Lyd we have hlyd = 'loud.' Yeo is the Saxon ea = 'water'."* This shows that interpretations can vary.

ROBOROUGH, of which there are two in Devon, means 'rough hill'. The village of Roborough near Plymouth used to be called 'Jump'.

ROCKBEARE, between Honiton and Exeter, means 'rook wood'.

ROMANSLEIGH takes its name from the dedication of its church to St Rumon.

ROSE ASH is a corruption of 'Rafe's Ash', after the family who once owned the manor.

ROWDEN appears many times in Devon and usually means 'rough hill'.

RUGGLESTONE INN is in the hamlet of Venton, a few hundred yards from Widecombe on Dartmoor. This unusual inn derives its name from an immense logan or rocking stone, which no longer rocks or rolls, on private land behind it. The Ruggle Stone, it was believed, could only be moved if the enormous key to Widecombe's church was placed into a crack in the rock.

ST GILES-IN-THE-HEATH, near Great Torrington, has, unsurprisingly, a church called St Giles and the latter part of the name was to differentiate it from 'St Giles in the Wood'.

SALCOMBE means 'salt valley'. Today it's packed with old yachting 'sea-salts'!

SALCOMBE REGIS, near Sidmouth, supposedly has royal connections for 'Regis' as added to Lyme, Bere and other places suggests this. It also helps to differentiate it from Salcombe, Devon's most southerly town.

SALTRAM ('Salterham' in 1249), is 'the home of the salt-workers'.

SAMPFORD COURTENAY, a once rebellious place near Okehampton, grew at 'the sandy ford' across the river Taw. The Courtenay family, Earls of Devon, owned land here from 1242.

SAMPFORD PEVERELL is another 'sandy ford'. Matilda Peverel held the manor in 1152.

SAMPFORD SPINEY is 'the sandy ford' over the Walkham and gives its name to the settlement on the hillside above it. It is named after an early landowner, Gerard de Spineto.

SANDFORD, near Crediton, possibly originates from yet another 'sandy ford', this time over a small tributary of the river Creedy. However, the Rev William Barter wrote this in 1755: *"So named, it being a sandy soil and at a ford at ye end of Churchtown"*.

SATTERLEIGH possibly means 'clearing of the robbers'.

SAUNTON, in North Devon, is probably 'the farm by the sands' and what sands they are!

SEATON, a modern resort in East Devon, means 'sea farm'.

SEVERN SEA is a preferred and more romantic name used by many as an alternative to the Bristol Channel and relates to the river of that name which broadens out into a sea.

SEWER MILL COVE, far more lovely than it sounds, is the only depression between Bolt Head and Bolt Tail. 'Sewer' is believed to derive from a Saxon word meaning 'sea-dwellers'.

SHALDON, opposite Teignmouth, possibly means 'on the shelf under the hill'.

SHAUGH PRIOR has two parts to its name. The first means 'rough wood' and the latter part underlines its ecclesiastical ties. It was given to the Prior of Plympton during the eleventh century.

SHEBBEAR is just possibly named after 'a wood which provided food and fuel'.

SHEEPWASH, in 1166 'Schepewast', famed for fishing, meant 'a place by the Torridge'.

SHELDON, in East Devon, is probably derived from 'the steeply shelving hill' which it's on.

SHERBORNE ROCKS lie just to the west of Beer Head in East Devon. Sherborne Abbey, in Dorset, once held extensive lands in Devon and also here at Beer, where its monks utilised nearby south-facing slopes to grow grapes for making wine. (Beer Wine?)

SHERFORD, near Kingsbridge, means a 'clear or bright ford'.

SHIRWELL, in North Devon, means 'clear spring', a good reason for settling!

SHOBROOKE, near Crediton, touches the supernatural because it means 'goblin brook'.

SIDBURY is 'the fort or castle above the River Sid'.

SIDMOUTH, sedate and sleepy, is at the mouth of the very short River Sid. It is possible that 'Sid' means 'wide' but generally speaking it isn't a big river in any sense, so the interpretation may relate to the width of the valley rather than the watercourse.

SILVERTON, although sounding like a simple enough name to explain, has provided plenty of food for discussion amongst academics far cleverer than me. The 'ton' is no problem for this is a farm. It's the 'Silver' bit that is a problem, as in 'Little Silver'. There are or were no silver mines like those at Combe Martin (a place which could have legitimately been called Silverton!). This was written in the *Devon & Exeter Gazette* in mid-April 1927: *"The Rev J. S. Hill, in his* Place Names of Somerset, *discusses the word 'Silver' as part of a place name and says that in connexion it is one of those words on which the speculation is endless. 'In the first place' he continues, 'we must note how widely dispread this name is, and so wide as to suggest that at least some of these names are more fancy names, and not of really ancient origin ... Silver, may be from several* sources, from, for instance, such a Scandinavian name as Solvar ... At least, in one instance Silver's-ton is explained as a mere shortening and popular corruption of St Silvanus. It is in Northamptonshire. Consequently only the history so far as ascertainable can help in the solution in each individual case." Just to add even more confusion, it may stem from 'Syle-ford-tun' meaning 'the farm by the miry ford'.

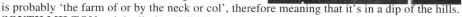

SLAPTON, in Start Bay, means 'slippery farm'.

SOURTON, on the north-western edge of Dartmoor, is probably 'the farm of or by the neck or col', therefore meaning that it's in a dip of the hills.

SOUTH MILTON, originally just 'Middleton', near Salcombe, means 'middle farm'.

SOUTH ZEAL, near Okehampton, is from the Saxon 'sell' meaning a 'dwelling'.

SOWTON, a small village near Exeter (and also the name of a sprawling industrial estate on the opposite side of the M5), probably means 'South farm'.

SOUSSONS is a large plantation, almost opposite the isolated Warren House Inn on Dartmoor. Its name probably means 'at the seven stones' but none remain, so far as is known.

SPARA BRIDGE spans the Teign near Ashton. It means something like 'a light bridge for crossing a river with high or steep banks' but this may refer to an earlier stone structure.

SPITCHWICK on Dartmoor might just possibly mean 'bacon farm' unless, of course, you can supply a rasher description!

SPREYTON, where Tom Cobley, of Widecombe Fair, reputedly lived, is just to the north-east of Dartmoor. The pub is named after him but most believe the Thomas Cobleigh buried near the church door was only a nephew. It's believed the village's name means 'farm in the brushwood'.

STADDON, fairly common in Devon, is believed to mean 'bullocks' hill'.

STARCROSS, on the Exe Estuary, is said to originate from times when those with a religious vocation landed here. It is believed a cross, on a flight of steps, attracted the name 'Staircross' for this place. It was 'Star Crosse' in 1689.

START POINT comes from the Saxon word 'steort' meaning 'a tail'.

STAVERTON, near Totnes, possibly means 'the village by the stony ford'.

STICKLEPATH, of which there are several in Devon, reflects the hilly nature of the county because it derives from the Anglo-Saxon 'sticele' meaning 'steep hill'.

STOCKLAND is believed to be 'land covered by sticks or stumps'. Now it has a TV mast!

STOKE when used in a place-name often means 'dairy farm'. However, the word has another root, an Old English word 'stoc' which means a monastic cell, e.g. Tavistock.

STOKE CANON, on the banks of the Culm, was 'Hirocastoc' in 938, the year the manor was given by King Athelstan to an Exeter monastery.

STOKE FLEMING was the homeland of the 'le Fleming' family in 1218.

STOKE GABRIEL is achieved by adding the name of the church, St Gabriel.

STOKEINTEIGNHEAD was the 'stoc' in the Ten Hides. (See **TEIGNHEAD**.)

STOKENHAM, near Start Bay, means 'the outlying farm in the meadows'.

STONEHOUSE, in Plymouth, takes its name from 'a stone house', built by 'Robert the Bastard' (no insult intended!) as a defensive strong point extending to Devil's Point.

STOWFORD probably originates from 'a ford marked by staves'.

STRETE means 'a surfaced road'. The one which now passes through is the A379 Dartmouth–Kingsbridge coast road. It used to be spelt 'Street' but so much mail went astray to Street in Somerset that, in the late nineteenth century, the last two letters were transposed.

SWILLY (North Prospect), a part of Plymouth, means 'gutter' or 'hollow place'.

SWINCOMBE, 'bright river', is a tributary of the West Dart.

TADDIFORDE is found in the St David's district of Exeter. It means 'toad-frequented ford'.

TADDIPORT, in North Devon, is 'toad town' but this is no reflection on the locals!

TALATON, in East Devon, is probably 'farm by the River Tale'. Tale means 'swift-flowing'.

TAMERTON FOLIOT, now part of the great urban sprawl of Plymouth, is 'the farm by the Tamar'. The Foliot family held the manor from 1242.

TAVISTOCK is the 'stoc' by the River Tavy.

TAW, the river which gives its name to many places, means 'silent one'.

TAWSTOCK, in North Devon, is 'the stoc farm by the Taw'.

TEDBURN ST MARY is about seven miles to the west of Exeter. The first part means 'Tetta's stream' and the rest is the church of St Mary.

TEIGNGRACE, near Newton Abbot, is by the Teign. Geoffrey Gras was there in 1352!

TEIGNHEAD appears in both Stokeinteignhead and Combeinteignhead, very long addresses for villagers to write. It is a corruption, partly influenced by the nearby river Teign, of 'Ten Hide'. This was an overall name for a collection of thirteen manors where the area, or hidage, amounted to Ten Hides, about 1200 acres.

TEIGNMOUTH is at the mouth of the Teign.

TEMPLER WAY is a 17-mile walk from the heights of Haytor to the coast at Shaldon. All along

this well-signed route are reminders of the great influence of the Templer family, who lived at Stover House, just outside Newton Abbot. This family owned the quarries at Haytor, built the Stover Canal and owned or traded on much of the land along the way.

TETCOTT, in West Devon, is 'Tetta's cot', no more, no less.

THELBRIDGE means 'plank bridge'.

THORVERTON is unusual in its place-name because it is probably Scandinavian in its origin and named after its founder. In 1340 it was 'Thurferton'.

THROWLEIGH is a lovely moorland village on Dartmoor. The first part of the name is believed to mean 'coffin'. Again the 'leigh' is believed to have been 'a clearing in wood'.

THRUSHELTON, to the north-west of Dartmoor, gives its name to the River Thrushel.

THURLESTONE takes its name from an isolated arched-shape sea-stack, formed of durable rock and called the Thurl Stone: that is, one with a hole! The rock, in an exposed location, has withstood some terrific storms and the locals say 'Brave every shock like Thurlestone Rock!' There is also a Thurlestone, which had this name in the thirteenth century, on Watern Tor on Dartmoor. This too has a gap, or 'thurl', through it.

TIVERTON derives from 'Twyford' where there were 'two fords' over two rivers, these being the Exe and the Lowman. It is not unusual for people with bad handwriting to have their correspondence arrive in Twerton, which is in Bath! Below, the town's name is spelt in flowers.

TOPSHAM comes from 'Toppa's Ham', the farm of Toppa.

TOPSHAM BRIDGE spans the Avon not far from Loddiswell. It is named after Richard de Toppesham, who held one 'ferling' of land in this parish in 1262.

TORBRYAN, in South Devon, was held by Wido de Brione in 1238. A tor is an outcrop of rock and there are many of these in this locality.

TORCROSS, in Start Bay, was associated with Walter de la Torre in 1281 and Adam de la Cros in 1316. It is possible that the 'tor' is the cliff outcrop above this small resort but there does not appear to be a cross here, the nearest being about a mile away.

TORQUAY was Torrekay in 1591, Torkey in 1715 and Tor Quay in 1765. It refers to the quay of Torre, attributed to the Premonstratensian monks of Torre Abbey who founded a settlement in 1196.

TORRIDGE is a lovely river, famous for Tarka the Otter, the creation, in the 1920s, of Henry Williamson. It derives from a Welsh word 'terig' which means 'rough or violent stream'. If in doubt ask some of the residents of Weare Giffard, who live on its banks.

TORS are common on Dartmoor and believed to derive from the Celtic 'twr' meaning tower.

TORY BROOK, which flows through the china-clay producing area on south-western Dartmoor to join the River Plym, also means 'rough or violent stream'.

TOTNES is an ancient borough on the lowest bridging-point of the Dart. The first part of the name is probably a personal one, Totta, whilst the second part, 'nes', means a 'nose' of land projecting into the valley.

TRENTISHOE, in North Devon, may mean 'circular hill' or 'the fort on the ridge'.

TRUSHAM, near Chudleigh, probably means 'farm in the brushwood'.

TYTHERLEIGH, in North Devon, is believed to mean 'thin woodland'.

TWINYEO is near Teigngrace and its name means 'between the waters'; in this case it is on the wedge of land at the confluence point of the rivers Bovey and Teign. Although the Teign is the greater river the depression where they meet is known as 'the Bovey Basin'.

TWITCHEN, on the southern edge of the Exmoor National Park, is believed to mean 'cross-roads' and there is a minor one in this small settlement.

TWO MOORS WAY is a long-distance footpath running from the southern side of Dartmoor at Ivybridge to Lynmouth on the northern side of Exmoor, a distance of just over 100 miles.

UFFCULME is 'Uffa's farm on the river Culm'.

UGBOROUGH, which is far prettier than its name suggests, means 'the fortified hill'. The first part is a personal name, probably that of the Celtic founder.

UNUSUAL NAMES, or evocative ones, are found on almost every map of Devon and here is just a small sample to find, and possibly interpret or research for yourself. (These are all genuine!) Affaland, Airy Point, Allaleigh, Alswear, Anchoring Hill, Anvil Corner, Arson, Assycombe Hill, Aunk, Backway, Bag Bear, Bagbeare, Baggy Point, Bald Hill, Balls, Ballsaddle Rock, Barricane Beach (famous for its shells), Beara Down, Beautiport, Beggar's Bush, Beggar's Roost, Ben Brook, Bendibus Hillcross, Bentwitchen, Beoples Barton, Bever Batch, Billhole, Bish Mill, Black Ball, Black Cove, Black Head, Blackness Rock, Blasteridge Hill, Bleak House, Blindwell, Bloody Pool, Bogtown, Boldventure, Bommertown, Boohay, Bosomzeal, Bottle Hill, Bottor Rock, Bowlish, Braddicksknap Hill, Brandy Cove, Breakneck Hole, Brithem Bottom, Broadall Gulf, Broadmoor, Brocks Common, Buckinghams Leary, Buckyette, Bugford, Bugle Hole, Bullhead, Bungsland, Bunson, Burnt House, Burston, Buskin, Buttis Pill, Buzzacott, Chasty, Chattafin, Cheglinch, Cholash, Cholch, Chumhill, Claw, Clickland, Cloggshill Cross, Coffins, Collipriest, Crankland Farm, Crapstone, Craze Lowman, Crock of Gold, Crooked Copse, Dabbs Moor, Damage Barton, the Dancing Beggars (which have sometimes seen a vowel changed!), Darlick Moors, Desolate, Devil's Elbow, Devil's Point, Devil Tor, Diddywell, Dippertown, Dipple, Dirks, Ditchett, Dog Village, Duntz River, Dux, Fairy Cross (not just slightly miffed?), Fancy, Fawns, Field Trish, Five Wyches, Flares, Floyte, Fluder & Foghanger, Folly Gate, Fosfelle, Friendship Farm, Frogmate Creek, Frogmore Creek, Fuidge, Gambuston, Gappah

(Goat's Path), Gingerland, Gittshayne, Godwell, Gogwell, Goodshelter, Great Seaside, Gribble Inn, Grunta Pool, Guzzle Down, Hanna Beth, Hansel, Hawns & Dendles, Hazard, Heiffers, Hens & Chickens, Herebere, Horralake, Horseyeat, Humble Point, Icy Park, Indio, Ingo Brake, Inner Hope, Inny Foot, Jack-in-the-Green, Jenny's Portion, Keyberry Copse (not Keystone!), Kingseat, Knackershole, Knotty Corner, Lickham Bottom, Little Comfort, Little Pillhead, Littlejoy, Loo Cross (no doubt placed for convenience), Lopwell Dam, Lovers Leap, Lythe-land, Marridge, Mine, Mockham Down, Money Acre Corner, Mount Folly, Mutterton, Nadrid, Neopardy, Noble Hindrance, Nutwalls, O Brook, Obsy, Off Cove, Outer Hope, Paradise Copse, Peacegate Cross, Piddledown Common, Piles (also Lower Piles and Higher Piles), Pinchaford, Pixies Hole, Pizwell, Place, Pludd, Pouncers, Pounces, Pratt's Hill, Providence Place, Redrot Cove, Riddlecombe, Risdon's Fishleigh, Rora Wood, Roundball Hill, Rubble Hills, Rubby Town, Ruddy Ball, Rughouse, Rugroad, Sanctuary Farm, Sanduck, Scouse Farm, Shadrack, Shop, Slymlakes, Snapper, Snow Ball, Sock Hill, Span Bottom, Spicelane, Spittle, Splat, Stinking Cove, Stony Corner, Stout Farm, Stretch Down, Stubborn, Summer, Swinesloose Farm, Tackbear, Tarbuddle, Toe Mills, Torbuddle, Trill, True, True Love, True Street, Trumps, Tuff Lane, Tumbling Hills, Twist, Volehouse, Whisselwell Farm, Wigley Cross (no way to win a 'Spot the Ball' newspaper competition!), Wisdome, and Wrinkley, which may be a good place for retirement … Let's end there!

UPLOWMAN is a settlement 'up the valley of the river Lowman'.

UPLYME, on the Devon/Dorset border, is a settlement 'up the valley of the river Lym'.

UPOTTERY is … , ok you have worked it out for yourself!

UPTON PYNE was the manor held by Herbert de Pynford in the thirteenth century. The first part of the name means 'higher farm'.

UTON, near Crediton, is 'the farm by the river Yeo'.

VALE OF DAWLISH appears to be a manufactured term, by geography teachers, to give a precise name to the area of market gardening found between the edges of Starcross and Dawlish. Locals tend to be unaware of this term and it doesn't feature on any maps that I have seen!

VENN OTTERY is a tiny settlement beside the Otter valley but slightly above the fen.

VIRGINSTOW is 'the holy place of the virgins'.

WALKHAMPTON gives its name to the nearby River Walkham. The name is possibly derived from 'wealca' which means 'the rolling river'.

WALLA BROOK as a tributary of the Dart means 'stream of the Britons' but as a tributary of the Avon is believed to mean 'brook fed by a spring', a liquid, rather than solid interpretation.

WARBOROUGH, found in several places, means 'a watch hill', one with a fine open view.

WARKLEIGH means 'spider wood', so you won't find me there!

WARREN is common in place-names on Dartmoor. The rabbit, bred in rabbit warrens or buries, was the staple diet of tin-miners. Therefore we have Ditsworthy Warren, Trowlesworthy Warren and so on. The Warren House, possibly the most famous pub on Dartmoor, has the symbol of the tinners – connecting rabbits' ears – above the door.

WASHBOURNE, a river in the South Hams, means 'sheep wash stream'.

WASHFIELD, near Tiverton, is possibly the 'open land by the low-lying marshland'.

WATCOMBE, now a part of Torbay, and famous for its clays means 'wheat valley'.

WEARE GIFFARD, pronounced 'Jifford', is on the banks of the Torridge and after prolonged spells of heavy rain is almost in it! Some of the houses have been raised to escape this watery problem. The first part of the name is self-explanatory. The Giffard family owned the land here until 1452 when the Fortescues acquired the estate.

WELCOMBE on the Devon/Cornwall border in NW Devon, possibly means 'spring valley'.

WEMBWORTHY may be 'a settlement on marshy ground'.